I0756012

FINISHING LINE PRESS
www.finishinglinepress.com

ALL THOSE WINDOWED ROOMS

poems by

Cathy Allman

Finishing Line Press
Georgetown, Kentucky

ALL THOSE WINDOWED ROOMS

ISBN 979-8-89990-484-4 First Edition

Publisher: Leah Huete de Maines
Editor: Christen Kincaid
Cover Art: Cathy Allman
Author Photo: Cathy Allman
Cover Design: Elizabeth Maines McCleavy

Order online: www.finishinglinepress.com
also available on amazon.com

Author inquiries and mail orders:
Finishing Line Press
PO Box 1626
Georgetown, Kentucky 40324
USA

Contents

"Then it struck me: Everything was a potential poem.
The stoic prayers of the mantis, the knowing
eyes of my dog..."

—Patti Smith

Outline for Her Novel

I. She wants to write about who she is as the heroine, but her mother creeps into the story. Her creator and her foil haunt every plot twist. She's trapped with her mother's character, eclipsing the beginning and pulling her back toward the place she's moved from.

II. When she speaks of her husband, she writes of the woman she is to him. It's important to her to be this woman: this homemaker, this lover, the mother of his children, his friend. That woman she writes about from her own point of view is a lovely lady who keeps house, and cooks, and she's funny, and she works out, and she got the kids through fine educations and into good marriages. She has friends. She has deep thoughts that she keeps between herself and the entity to whom she prays. She fills daily blank pages with questions.

> A.
>
> But if she writes about herself from his point of view, she's critical. She objects to his habit of not courtesy flushing. She doesn't like the way he piles projects on his desk or doesn't wipe his fingerprints from the counter. She takes offense to the fact that when he feeds the dog chicken, he helps himself to some of the dark meat and skin—a bite for the dog, a bite for him. She doesn't like to watch him pick meat from the bones with his greasy fingers. She wants his portion on a plate, with silverware, napkin, and conversation.

III. And if she tells you about her children, she can't tell you what they think of her, the way they were unhappy that she made them build snowmen in the backyard so that the front yard stayed unblemished. When they bring this up, they laugh. She explains that the front yard is where the septic fields are, and she didn't want them eating snow that might have groundwater seepage. And that's not a lie. But they aren't wrong. She liked the snow without footprints.

> A.
>
> She can't tell you about how they felt driving themselves to school, where their thoughts were, how they felt about merging into rush-hour traffic. She doesn't know how safe they felt when she was behind the wheel. She only knows she

was afraid of some collision from a blind spot. Even if it wasn't her fault, there'd be damage.

IV. She doesn't see herself when trying to write these stories.

A.
She doesn't see what other people notice: the gap in her teeth, the gray at the roots of her hair, that sometimes she squints and has an expression that might look like disdain. Often her smile could appear forced. Her children called it her perma-smile. They never had reason to understand her superpower of smiling. They had no idea about her relationship with pretending.

B.
They do tell her their feelings. She knows when they're nervous, knows how they talk their way into finding the positive, of keeping track of the good. She likes to think she passed on, by example, the vision of process, the possibility for change. But does she lie to herself? Does she try to focus on good when she writes in order to not mention the things that are wrong? The mold under the sink where the spray hose leaked; the corner of the garage where the drywall stayed wet and needs replaced. The fact that her daughter-in-law doesn't like her and her son-in-law thinks she's silly.

V. On a sunny day, you'd never guess that when it rains hard all the water rolls down the hill and turns the bend to saturate her front lawn and pools in her driveway. When it rains hard, she wanders in the runoff without boots. She carries a shovel, cursing, trying to unclog leaves from the drains.

A Life Review: Four Stars

In the film version of my life, based on my found journals,
you cast Geena Davis as me. Really?
When I was writing myself,
I always saw Michelle Pfeiffer playing the part.

I get why you gave Clint Eastwood the story to direct,
a *Bridges of Madison County* thing, right?
I love the way Clint plays songs I wrote
on the piano throughout the film.
I just never saw myself
as that lonely, defiant, or trapped to the point
that any choice I could make
would only be the best choice
of a no-win decision.

Living the story, I was under
the impression I won.

Tom Hanks is an inspired choice for your father.
You captured the truth of how hard
he and I worked to hang on.

Which one of you was the genius
who realized all those years of my being invisible
could (with the aid of special effects)
prove invisibility is a superpower?

This is the season boats return

to this river, currents glimmer.
I walk like the ghost
of what I once wrote
in sidewalk chalk.

I stare where sun bleeds
between an elder canopy
of new oak and maple.
I wonder now, more than wait
while these fast days finish,

and the world runs ahead.
I'm someone's
grandmother in flat shoes
and cropped white pants.
I amble leashed to my dog,

and start to bleed
where I cut my shin on thorns.
I notice new freckles,
and darker moles spot my ankle.
They were not there

when I was smooth-skinned
and smelled like soap.
In the world of *next*,
I miss what I already grieve.

Imagined Future

We dressed up in our mothers' stained
negligées, with their missing buttons
and moth-eaten lace robes,
strutted on top of the cement
retaining wall that delineated
the steep change of elevations.
My mother's worn kitten heels
didn't fit us, one wrong step drew
blood, tore her hand-me-down gown.
And when it rained,
we pulled out our suitcases
of alter-egos and plastic pumps.
I wanted to be Barbie's cousin Francie—
Francie Fairchild. Flat-chested, with bangs.
I wasn't the star. That was my friend
Jackie's job. I wasn't even the star's sister—
I was cousin in our make-believe kingdom.
My Ken was tall and strong and without
male parts. I guided my perfect pair
to their pretend cocktails.
They wore zipper-less evening clothes
and traveled in a cherry red Corvette
that twisted and turned over
the invisible road along the fringe
of my bedroom rug. We giggled
behind the door closed to parents—
played at what we expected
grown-up would be.

She Thought the Camera Loved Her

What his camera captured
was squarely framed. The black-
and-white developed into a woman
who had her bone structure,
long legs, wind-blown hair,
faded jeans and wide eyes.
Her broken parts escaped his shot.
She kept those to herself
the way she still does.
Good subject, good student,
good practice but she never learned
f-stops, lenses, the science of light
or the camera craft of their film school.
She had trained to be on screen.
He majored in cinematography.
When, too many decades later,
she was surprised by the ghost
of his name as credits rolled,
something inside her singed
by the dredged-up scald
and scorched stench
of feathers and wax wings
so close to the sun
above the Hollywood sign.

Untraveled

I miss your banjo strum. You didn't know
I listened when I fussed and dipped chicken into egg,
coated the white meat of our dinner
with crushed cornflakes, heated our frozen
succotash and Poppin' Fresh rolls.

I think about dinner and watching *Cosmos*:
"For small creatures such as us, the vastness
is only bearable with love," Carl Sagan said. We
had hunger and questions, wanted answers
from gravity and unknown galaxies, and cheap

wine. We made love on the floor before
the show ended. I missed your call
the next day at my cubicle, where I was careful
that car ads didn't run in the same two-minute break.
I replayed your voicemail apologies.

And this many years past that meteor
of us, the crash, the burn, the cold rock and dust,
I wonder who our children would've been,
in what city our vacation home, what stories
you never got to tell me about lacerations you stitched,

or hearts you restarted, or babies you pulled
into this earth. I re-imagine places you took me
on the back of your Harley, without a helmet
just leaning with each bend, wind-tangled hair,
dust flew while we rumbled over back roads,
places no one knew.

About the Life You Imagine for Yourself

You live with pantries of expired food,
a refrigerator with moldy cheese,
frost on the imported coffee ice cream,
and only one day left until the milk sours.

Only weeks ago, it was humid and bright.
The porch light doesn't work
even though you changed the bulb.
You replaced the smoke alarm batteries

the way you're supposed to
when daylight savings is over.
You sleep through the hour gained.
The flashlight is a small weapon against the moon,

and your glass of wine a tiny defense against
what? When you had it, whatever that *it* was,
you thought you were
too fat or your kids wouldn't listen

or your husband worked too much
or you didn't work enough.
You've moved to Florida
just because you're tired of snow.

The thing is, there's stuff you live with
that's over and gone. What you believed
was *so long* turned into *farewell.*

Not in the Wonder Box

Sand tray therapy allows a person to construct
his or her own microcosm using miniature toys
and colored sand.
—from goodtherapy.org

My tray would be a desert.
I'd rake the grit with my fingers

into waves like wind makes,
dig rivulets where water ran,

like traces from rain.
There would be no mountains.

I wouldn't use those plastic dinosaurs,
toy soldiers, the sculpted

polar bear with cub.
I wouldn't use the dolls

from the pink house, not even
the dog. The figures posed in the box

would be cut flowers—
finite, green leaves that take light,

feed buds, burn to orange,
lose petals, turn to dust.

In Another Life

Sometimes at 2 a.m. your ghost slips into my bed
through the slumbering realm between my husband and my nightmares.

There, I tell you about my garden, sleepwalk with you through the French doors
admiring my pool inside the white picket fence below my bedroom balcony.

In that moment there are no scars, or complex fractures, no limping,
just dancing barefoot beneath the fountain's warm splashing

water washing away all the unspoken, unfinished, unanswered
empty spaces and blood. See those red roses climbing the trellis?

In another life I will be the one who says, "No matter what, I'll always love you."
You will be the one who drives your station wagon into a wall.

I will sit at your bedside viewing you through tubes and ask, "What happened?"
You will wonder where to begin, why you didn't wear a seat belt.

You will be unable to find words through a morphine-hazed dream.
You will feel like it is time for some final exam, but you can't find the building.

I will disappear, marry someone else, and pretend you never happened.
You will divorce the person you left me for.

I will be glad you left me, I mean, left the me you never actually got to know.
I will get to really see myself instead of looking in the mirror at your shadow.

I will not wrestle with the life we never finished living,
the life the palm reader on Melrose told us would be happily ever after.

Wonder Woman

I was a volunteer acting coach
on Monday nights at a teen group home
where residents had confidential manila folders
that I wasn't cleared to read. For all I knew,
the girls were like the private students I'd taught.
They sat in blue jeans and t-shirts in a circle
on the stained shag rug. I had no real
microphone, but with my fingers
wrapped around emptiness, the nothing inside
my fist was the pretend into which they answered
my news reporter question—*Tell me*
about your superpowers? I asked
like a real helmet-haired newscaster.
The girls weren't faster than a speeding bullet
or able to leap tall buildings in a single bound,
but for our one hour, they declared they had magic
mirrors, and time travel watches.
I can cure sickness with a single kiss.
And the next day on my drive
to my real job, scheduling TV commercials,
my thoughts were lost to the class,
where whoever tuned in to listen, heard,
I make flowers grow through concrete with tears.

Through the Looking Glass

Poem in response to Girl Before a Mirror
by Pablo Picasso 1932. Oil on canvas.

What happens when the side that breathes
pulls herself into the side that is glass?

On one side, a feather fills where hair would fall
on the full-faced figure baring breast, heart and womb.

Black and white stripes form a spine.
A segmented arm with white fingers reaches through the blue.

Both halves share ribs of blood and black bone.
On the darker side the dream bleeds.

Looking outside her reflection, the lone eye cries to a half moon.
The transgression of the side from light hides a green heart.

Oval orange framing covers a white, shadowed halo.
The mirror image waits in robes of sapphire with purple lining.

Shapes and silence side by side until
transcending the glass darkly the other turns face to face.

Meditation Before the Time Changes

Naked branches dangle white sheets
as pretend ghosts. The dog and I walk
through the storm of time change.
Each day we pace our same route,
with different suns. Daylight shortens
as darkness expands. Leaves twirl
through the dusk, impossible to catch,
when I try to snag one from the path of a gust.
The burn of florescent luminous yellow,
orange, and the red-veined oak offers
brilliant color for emptiness. Gutted pumpkins
flame from inside. Plastic bones pose
as skeletons on mailboxes and stone fences.

In from the cold, I wait to answer.
I make a fire in the hearth before I open the door
to each ring. My dog barks. The haunters
collect treats I parcel. Some even say, *Thank you.*
I watch as they run across the street.
Acorns crunch under their shoes.
The night whirls. Tomorrow is All Saints' Day.
I will pray to candles, kneel to statues.
Sculpted images know tombstone stillness.
Silence knows the answer to prayer.

Lost Along the Way

I

I had a child's necklace
with a mustard seed inside
a plastic hourglass.
But I remember standing in my bedroom,
our first move, the room empty, the closet bare,
the curtainless window
with a numinous stream of sun.
On my hands and knees, I crawled
to every unfurnished corner, ran my hand
over the dusty floor, thinking the hourglass
that I couldn't see in the dark would be found
after everything it could have hid underneath
had been removed.

II

In our new home, I lost my child body to breasts.
I lost the feeling that my parents loved each other.
I lost the gift to play with boys without worrying
that they might try to kiss me.

III

I lost the notion of just running around the track
to the notion of winning a race
to the notion of beating my last time
to the notion that someone was chasing me
to the notion that I couldn't let them pass.

IV

I lost living in my parents' house,
I lost being home at midnight
to kissing Aaron in our dorm.
l lost hiding behind a chair
during their name-calling fights
to letting my boyfriend feel me up.
I lost their excuses for why problems
couldn't be solved
to my own mysteries
to my own reasons.

V
I lost Paul to an actress he photographed,
that he'd always loved, though
she didn't love him. He hung the framed shot
above his bed. I closed my eyes to love him.
He lost his parents' marriage to his father's
bi-plane and his mother's fear of flying.
First, he said to me, *You're crazy,*
then he said, he never said he loved me.
I believed him.

VI
I lost my track career to a brick wall
when I crashed my car—
lost my unbroken skin and bones
to blood, screws, stitches and scars.

VII
I lost my maiden name to my husband
or just gave it up.
I lost my paying job to diapers and carpool or maybe
to the moves for my husband's corporate climb.

VIII
I lost our children to engagement rings,
weddings, prospects in other cities.

IX
I lost my father
to Parkinson's dementia.
I lost my mother to denial.
I lost Florida to his dying.
I lost my fear of old age.
I say, *It's all for a reason.*
I lost my rationalizing
to believing,
and even if I never found it,
my mustard seed grew.

Female in a Bot Marriage

She chooses a game-ready
cyber representative
that has everything
her fleshy self never had.
Then the start button is pushed.
The game is on.
She finds herself lying,
manifested,
next to a green metallic male being.
Despite her previous design efforts,
she ends up green too.
She has become cleverly assembled
into the image of his forever companion.
She battles, but
never speaks.
She battles, but
her bot experiences no pain.
No bones break.
Just shattering sound blips
of clanking and clashing.
No scars show.
No discernible expressions.
No altercation elicits even one tiny tear
as she moves time-trapped through
her fixed-size graphic area,
all data coded, compressed, and decoded,
bleeding red eight-bits-per-pixel blobs.
She is animated, destroyed,
reanimated, destroyed, reanimated,
destroyed, reanimated,
achieving each next, more
accomplished level.
Her cyber-steely
alter-ego burns and bends,
until she drops her joystick.
Soda spills.
The game stops beneath the glass.

Stockholm Syndrome

My husband wandered
to the grill aisle, while I perused
lamps. I carried a broom
and fertilizer and tried
to find him. Every man,
down every aisle, had gray hair,
Bermuda shorts, t-shirt, ball cap,
and round belly, but they weren't him.

We're building our forever
home before the assisted living years.
My decorator sends me designs—
all chrome and mid-century
modern. I want a fireplace. She says,
It's Florida—you don't need the heat.

I tell her I like old things—
wood and chandeliers with crystal.
I'm okay with tarnished brass.
I need my coffee tables to endure
wet glass rings, hot mugs.

This millennium skews modern,
stays ahead of the curve—albeit retro.
But gravity to me, in these years,
is not forward momentum.
I accept where things sag
or tear, I ignore chipped paint—
all the evidence of damage,
and the thief who ransoms my time.

I Can't Tell You Why

plays on the radio
as we drive to Mass. Late, we turn it off
as the Eagles sing, *Aren't we the same two*
people who lived through years in the dark?

Inside, sun streams through stained glass,
taints your blue shirt with yellow light.
There are peonies, roses in front of the altar—
there must have been a wedding.

Parishioners recite, *I confess to almighty God.*
I mumble the words by rote
and think of my father at our wedding.
Her mother and I do, he said, then put my hand in yours.

I move my hand near yours on the pew without touching,
recall when you said the same thing at our daughter's
wedding. I'm looking more at the bowls of flowers
than at the Savior nailed to the marble cross above.

The priest in the pulpit reads with his brogue
about disciples asking Jesus if he was Elijah,
when Jesus asked Peter, *Who do you say I am?*
The sermon's disjointed; my mind drifts to your
retirement party, colleagues, the stories
thanking you for your generosity, the lives
you lifted, how you'll be missed.

I hold your hand while we deliver the Lord's prayer,
squeeze your fingers at *Forgive us our trespasses.*

When we drive through oak-lined streets
to our favorite diner, I almost ask you,
Who would you say I am?
but I don't want to know your answer.

We eat fried eggs and English muffins
every Sunday after church. I dip toast
in the gooey yolk. The waitress brings coffee,
hovers over my almost empty cup, and asks,
Would you like more?
Yes. Please.

You Don't See Me, But I Hear You

If my husband were a landscape,
he'd be a golf course. He'd have water hazards
and sand traps, fairways, and greens
with changing degrees of difficulty.

In our house, he likes to dwell in his office
or in front of his barbecue or big screen.

If I were a landscape, I'd be a forest bordered
by fern, wild rose, clover, and honeysuckle.
I'd have wetlands and a creek that runs
with varying depths, depending on the tide.

I abide in the kitchen and garden.
We share the same bed, sleep, but have different dreams.

I've lived in a parallel universe,
occupied space designed for another person.

My bitmoji is a one-dimensional cartoon woman
with bobbed hair and black glasses,
the kind of person who doesn't say much,
but what she does say is over-encouraging.
I hear you, man.

To help with my husband's hearing loss,
phone calls go directly
into the Bluetooth speaker in his ear.
When he closes his office door, I still hear him.
The cadence of his conversations, moments of silence
met with thoughtful responses, directions.

I can't help but be skilled at eavesdropping,
immersed in peripheral banter, even on trains
or in restaurants, like a fly in the seat behind you.

My father was a salesman, my brother as well.
I'm a bit of a salesman's dream—
I'll buy it.

Outtakes from Happily Ever After

I

My husband and I watch a TV show called *State of the Union.*
The wife, who wants a divorce, asks the husband
on a scale of one to ten, *How unhappy will you be if we divorce?*

My answer is ten. The TV wife pauses, finally says, *Seven.*

II

I've played this character a long time.
The persona I play answers to his last name.
My maiden name only exists on papers from before 1984—
a newspaper clipping of my high school honor roll
or the Google roster of my college track team from the '70s.
I still have a box of old business cards,
despite the too many other things I've thrown away.

If we were a Netflix series, I'd know the lines for my part
as his wife in *The Mystery of Us.* I'd get written-by credit.
My salt-and-pepper hair would be exactly the same
of that of the protagonist, our children's mother.
I researched the backstory for my role as my mother's daughter.
I've been cast as this woman longer than anyone on *Law and Order*,
longer than Vanna has been on *Wheel of Fortune.*

III

I am a rerun in syndication.
When given a cameo in the new episodes,
my character wears a surgical mask, but I can't stay in character.
I'm not the part I'm playing. My recurring character
has a grown daughter who mocks this mother
for her past record of carbohydrate-intense meal plans.
Evidence: mashed potatoes, stuffing, boxed macaroni and cheese.
The menu/rap sheet is several pages.

IV

I prefer reruns. They are less frightening—mild, nostalgic,
but they likely scared me when they first aired. When lost
in plot-watching, I make a note of how many of the actors
are no longer alive, they visit my screen like clockwork.
I pick up the clues easily. Is that because I've already seen it,
or because I pay close attention now with the closed caption
running underneath the picture? If my husband walks in
on me watching *Flip or Flop*, he says, *I have trouble figuring out*
if Tarek and Christina are still married. Those two
TV personalities haven't aged, but they've matured
in ways they hadn't grown before their divorce.

V

When they rerun *Antique Road Show,*
they caption/postscript the segment,
with the appraised-for-insurance-purposes value.
If you had sold it ten years ago... the expert says to trigger regret
about Aunt Libby's vase. But Aunt Libby's niece
couldn't have known.

Not Found in Obituaries, Eulogies, Fairy Tales or the Book I Haven't Written

I've had resumés, photos, children, a home, a dog, a routine—all kinds of witnessable expressions of this aging being who continues to subsist within this body who answers to my name.

I keep trying to capture sunrises in photos, the way the clouds and sky spark a fire but only for the briefest of moments, and then the empty atmosphere between earth and space is all blue or grey or some cold color with no shade of red.

I puzzle through my own childhood, sifting memories. Do I think if I stack the episodes in just the right sequence, I'll find an answer, algorithm, some semblance of science that gives proof and therefore: truth?

Truth with a capital *T* is what I was told is the word, the Bible. How many times does the Bible ask: *He who has eyes, let him see. He who has ears, let him hear?* I googled a website with fifty-six verses with some form of that question. That verse appears in both the New Testament and the Old Testament. Fifty-six quotes and still not the answer to my question.

Every Night, I'm Lying in Bed Holding You Close in My Dreams

We drive over snow, my husband and I,
skidding glazed roads, seat heaters and defrosters
on full blast—luxury heat features
cannot beat the absolute power
of polar vortex and the sub-zero.
Then *The Best of My Love* rises
from the radio. I sing along, every word
in sync with 1980 when my boyfriend
was about to leave without a reason
he'd share, no mention of the nurse
he commiserated with about her engagement
to the wrong man. I know who I was that year—
all goopy and not-formed like a chicken
still in the egg, not ready to crack the shell,
only ready enough for a Styrofoam carton
in the grocery cooler. I sing the sweet words
of being wrong while my husband pulls
us into our garage. I want him to leave the car on—
I don't want him to close the door,
just let the music finish,
yet we unlock our home of twenty-three years instead.
I unload groceries, pour wine,
light a fire and hear
the pedal steel lift above the twelve-string
over and over in my head.

My Inner Neil Armstrong

I used a crowbar to open
the handed-down cedar chest
and found the 1969

National Geographic moon photos
in a pile with your letter
to the younger me.

Inside the space capsule,
astronauts checked figures,
twisted dials, like they rehearsed.

Your letter read:
I know you've started a new life
and may still hate me
for ending our relationship

The crew's gauges synced
to math, to the flight plan.

as I did, but I'd like to keep in contact
with you no matter how infrequent.
You're a good person

The space explorers exited
what keeps Earth spinning—
gravity and atmosphere.

and you know how rare
good people are on this coast
(in the movie business especially).

Mission control played Sinatra,
"Fly Me to the Moon,"
and Streisand's "People Who Need People."

I hope and pray
(yes, occasionally)
that you are happy.

On the dark side of the moon,
space is radio silent, except
for its reckoning of jet propulsion.

I won't mention marriage,
but if it happens,
you should let me know,

The Eagle has landed
one small step for man,
footprints on the lunar surface.

so I can change the name
on this envelope.

Debate for the Exact Word

...it was her poem and she herself up against
that gymnasium wall, and it felt like love,
and the hell with all of us.
—from "Decorum," by Stephen Dunn

And the time I said it felt like love
there on the beige, coarse carpet
TV blaring nonsense nightly news behind us.
Two unfinished puddles of mashed potatoes
and chicken bones waited to be cleared.
Not eaten, because we weren't that kind
of hungry.
And the time I said, it felt like desperation
your shirt unbuttoned, my jeans unsnapped.
Your knees, my elbows rug burned.
You left your boots on.

And then after, unwrinkled, reclasped,
presentable and tidy, I returned
to the stainless-steel sink, scraped
leftovers into the trash, squirted blue
dish soap on black cast iron—scrubbed,
dried, put away pans and continued
to view that seventies war, which was
reported on screen every night
while I didn't pay attention.

Why, out of all the lovemaking or
fucking or whatever reptilian
consumption of one another
we engaged in, do I label
that night as love?

What name would you give it?

The Fire We Spin Around

You were young, and after three Jacks
he said he loved you.
He touched you awake in places you didn't know.

Decades later, the same man after three Jacks
tells you everything wrong
with life is because of you.

You can't sleep, and he won't remember.
You hear his irregular breathing,
replay the weeks of his chemo.

An owl calls from a tree.
The clock on the nightstand
ticks on, like years.

The next-door neighbor has Alzheimer's.
The caretakers flame her floodlight all night long.
That fluorescence slices between the bottom

of your pulled-down shades and the sill.
The house that holds the body of the woman
whose mind has left has stumps of fallen trees.

Poison ivy intermingles with English along
the overgrown border of ground cover.
Her damaged windows need to be replaced.

The pane fog looks like frost-crusted glass.
The quiet between her house and yours is so loud
you wonder what the silence wants to say.

Truth, Beauty and Photoshop

She was born in a delta
of three rivers. He'd been a native
of that river which had caught fire.

But physics is not biology.
Equal and opposite reactions
happen between two bodies.

Their past dissolved into next,
torn like a lost lotto ticket,
scattered as a broken strand of pearls.

Their wounds trailed like the wake of a trawler.
They argued through that slipstream of eras
and ages, cities and places they tried to call home.

And yet, each next morning while they walk,
she aimed another attempt to compress
the radiance of sunrise with a snapshot.

Later, on her laptop,
she added light, deepened color
to her ever-changing obligatory daily photo,

but the beauty never matched After Effects.
After edit attempts, like clockwork,
she once more clicked: *Restore to original.*

The Notion of Being Prepared

I think of old friends in California
shaken out of bed at 4 a.m.
Get out, firefighters scream.

The winds are eighty mph, and with flames
at that speed, there's no time
to prepare, only run.

After the firestorm passes,
stare at what once was
a mansion—you came from ash,

to ash you return.
I'm not ready for Christmas,
nor to go up in a conflagration.

I don't want to look at the things
about myself I need to change.
I've made space in the closet

of my soul for my sins as outdated
as prom dresses, crisp white blouses
I might need again, they still fit,

souvenirs of who I was
as if who I am is a question
with one answer:

a eulogy from a fortune cookie,
an ad agency slogan,
a motto, a mantra, a tweet—

something short, catchy, memorable,
a caption of clarity,
of a present that has passed.

Recovery Teacher

I
In the psych ward it's bright and clean at the table
where they write. The windows look out on a frozen,
crystal-covered lawn. Silent white falls
while their pencils scratch along evenly spaced lines
their unspoken squalls on paper.

II
She doesn't know how a patient arrives
at this place. They don't know why
she teaches here. There are assumptions.

III
Out the window she watches fog hover.
The air is too cold for evaporation—
part snow, part wet air. She sees
what doesn't vanish dangle.

IV
She writes while they write.
They won't hear about the wall she hit
asleep at the wheel. Boots hide the scars
where the tibia broke through her skin
and the surgeon sliced to put in the screw.
A discolored cord of tissue
still bracelets half of her ankle.

V
In this room, she's neither artist nor art.
She's the wall; a blank place pieces hang.
She's eyes and ears without mouth.
She can't teach what she doesn't know.

VI
What she knows of an unquiet mind,
she learned from her dead father,
sometimes haunted.
She doubts the truth of her memory—

confuses antagonist with protagonist.
She writes. Pronouns blur.
She revises.

Pittsburgh as a Metaphor for My Father

My father was no stranger to factory life,
or the toxic biproducts spilled into the Allegheny
from making glass, steel, the river he swam in as a child.
He was a realist, no matter how much superstition
the stories in his childhood mass-produced.
My father, like his mother, like his father-figures
from the volunteer fire department next to their row house
had worked in the factory. He pushed large plates
of glass from the assembly line to where they were cut,
then transported. If the glass dropped, there was blood.
Mindless, but he had to keep alert to the delicacy
of the manual labor. My father had his drinks at the bar
after his shift ended or at the fire department where the guys
told dirty stories, and he'd think of becoming a Cadillac salesman,
dream of wearing white shirts. He gave me a glamorous view
of fossil fuel when he sold for Eastern Coal. He explained
that without coal there wouldn't be electricity, or steel. He explained
how coal was formed by prehistoric forests buried by floods,
and time, and soil deposited over what used to be plant life
until enough heat converted trapped carbon
covered by peat bogs into coal. And I knew, that if coal stayed
in the ground long enough, for many millennia, un-mined,
the next step in the pressure transformation would be diamond.
He didn't just sell tonnage, one time my father sold an abandoned
mine,
he turned a profit off the unused. And Pittsburgh in those days was as
dirty
as people used to think it was, smoke billowing so thick
that if you hung your white laundry on the clothesline out to dry
and didn't bring it in quickly the soot would stick, sheets weren't white
anymore.

Born to Pittsburgh

I sat with him bedside,
forty years after his last drink
just the day before he'd look at me
and say, *This dying is hard.*
All I could hear
was his breath and the big band
my laptop leaked into the unsaid.

His Pittsburgh self used to tell me,
"I have clay feet." He didn't want
me to forget there were parts
we left out. Years we didn't talk about—
words he'd been too drunk to remember.

Now when I exercise on machines
with springs, straps and tools of resistance
all to make myself stretch
farther than I can alone,
farther than father, but I see him
in my toes, my feet, smaller,
but shaped like his.

Mutated World Sequence

I

When I was a girl, I watched *Let's Make a Deal.*
No one could know what was behind the boxes,
or curtains, or in Monty Hall's pockets.
Contestants had to choose without knowing—
lucky or unlucky, it was a game of chance.
I wanted the contestants to be lucky;
a prize could change their life.
I wanted to be lucky.

II

When I was a baby, my mother won
a powder blue Plymouth station wagon
from a fire department raffle.
We needed the car.
She fainted when she got the call.
The kitchen phone dangled
as my mother lay on the floor.
My father accepted the prize.

III

One afternoon, my mother left me
alone in the vehicle of her good fortune.
She says I released the emergency brake.
The car rolled down the hill into a tree.
The distance traveled didn't have enough
time or space for momentum.
Neither the car nor the toddler I was
were damaged. My mother sprained her ankle
when she ran to catch us. She repeats
the story of how she got hurt.

IV

My father quoted his Bible—
Maltz's *Psycho-Cybernetics.*
Cybernetics, loosely translated from Greek,
is "a helmsman who steers his ship to a port."

My father always wanted to get out
of his factory life—become a white-collar worker.
He admired the used car salesmen.
He pictured himself clipped in crisp collars and ties.

My father explained that the brain doesn't know
the difference between what you do and what you imagine.
They train, but athletes rehearse winning in their minds,
visualize until it feels real, like a dream.

Detours

I drove past my exit on I-95 again,
the second time this week.

I'm frightened. I talk to the part
of myself at the wheel when I veer

off at 17 when I meant to take
the off-ramp at 16. Where am I?

How'd I get here? I turn around.
There is chatter in my mind along

my route although I drive alone.
I pass familiar landmarks

alone but in conversation
with the woman I was another

time on this road. I'm like a film
where the soundtrack is out of sync

with the lip movements. Dialogue
entertains and advances the story,

but someone else narrates,
commentates, watches while

I'm at the wheel in conversation
with remembered questions

and imagined tomorrows. I turn
back, re-enter the highway in the right

direction. Be patient. I tell both
the driver and the critic.

I think of the green, blue and yellow stick
family held up with magnetic letters

on my refrigerator, and it triggers the memory
of the white board on my father's door—

with *Today is Tuesday. It's ninety degrees.*
Lunch is turkey sandwich and apple pie.

My father told me how good
his sugar-free apple pie tasted.

He said he loved me. He said,
Thank you. I say thank you back to the memory.

I'm flooded with scrambled recollections.
I'm tired of all the no outlet cul-de-sacs

I turned onto by accident,
the streets of houses I didn't buy,

the addresses of homes I sold.
Familiar haunts no longer there—

morphed into a phone store
or yoga studio or luncheonette.

For a moment I'm lost.
The next minute, I'm in a hurry.

In the end, I'm not there yet.
At the red light, again immersed in nostalgia

I explain to the fairytale—the movie star
I dressed up as from the trunk

beside my childhood cardboard kitchen—
I say, *Trick or treat, Sleeping Beauty,*
the years have wrapped sweetness.

My Father: Here, Not Here

I slogged along the steady surf
my heavy steps sunk in sand,
when evening began.
It seemed that fleeting flame
of bruised light was my father.

Between a rock and high rise
I tossed a feather
and a broken shell into the Gulf—
wordless prayers
for the living and the dead.

Back inside his room, his bifocals rested
in a tray with pennies and paper clips.
His windbreaker
back on the door hook.
I switched on his lamp,
and waited in that glow.

Zero-Sum Game

My hairdresser Sophia from Morocco told me
about two angels in Islam.
One keeps a tally of good, the other of evil.

When she spun my chair toward the mirror,
she told me about the line
all must cross, "The path is thinner than a hair."

And what I think of is my father, who kept
a ledger under the kitchen sink
between the dish soap and drain cleaner.

On the left column he'd drawn a stick figure
with wings and a halo; on the right
a figure with horns and a pitchfork.

Last night I woke in another cold sweat
with secrets I've written, small details
I told myself no one would ever see—

Thanksgivings with gin gimlets
instead of gratitude. Fear
that my father would wake up

angry, so drunk he'd piss in the closet.
I was young. He kept score.

Email to My Dead Father

Today, when I told Mom I'm afraid
to administer the syringe of insulin
to my dog, she said, *I never thought*
I'd have to inject my husband.
And presto—there you are, in the car
with us as I drive her to the hair salon.
I don't remember her giving you shots.
I saw you do it to yourself hundreds
of times, but she said that was her.

Then, she asked me to take her to Walmart.
She's slow with her walker. The sun is hot.
The parking lot reflects, the black top amplifies heat.
I shuffle beside her aware that we're blocking
other shoppers. She either doesn't see, or doesn't care
about our existence as obstacles. She spent
much too long in each aisle, asked me
to read small print, relay price per ounce.
The incontinence supply rack
and the feminine itch cream shelf
made me wish I could disappear.

I heard your voice in my thoughts, *Oh Patty, hurry up.*
Oh Patty, you don't need that.
Oh Patty, you won't leave until the last bitch...

I can't remember the end of that quote.

I google, get a bunch of rap songs,
not what you used to say.

In the car, on the way back to her senior living apartment
I told her that my neighbors are moving to Idaho.
Idaho? she said.

The neighbors said they don't like living on a golf course.
They read online that Idaho has good bike trails.
Remember Dad's joke? She nodded,

looked side-eyed at me from the passenger seat.
We smiled more from nostalgia, than from humor.

I hate watching Mom fade.
Dad, you'd hate how the world's changed.

The Morning My Father Moved into Assisted Living

He asked me to help him shave, even though
as his daughter, we never had that rite of passage—
father teaching son to use a razor.

He sat in front of the sink with his shirt off,
the long scar up his belly from the surgery
he had as a baby in 1929, still deep and present.

He sprayed foam onto his hand, patted
the cream over his cheeks, chin, above his upper lip,
left the water running to rinse off clipped stubble.

He tackled one section at a time, like the way he used to
shovel snow from our driveway one shovel full
after another for hours while the snow wouldn't stop.

And I remember how methodically he'd mow
the lawn strip by strip into green straight stripes.
Many things I watched, but my father never taught me.

He kept tending to the task at hand: remove
a patch of bristle, rinse the sharp edge, repeat.
Me invisible, but ready to help with what he couldn't reach.

I wasn't observing the blade to the skin,
I was noticing my father's gaze into his blue eyes
in the mirror, I wondered who he saw each morning.

I stared into those eyes too. This man I stood behind
had watched a half-century of my life with different
clean-shaven faces. I couldn't look away.

Writing the Part of Her Father

Abandoned, he'd answered
to the surname of a ghost.
But to her, he was
many men—some good,
some less so. She told herself
to love them all.

When she wrote her father's bio
as hero, she lied a little.
When she delivered his eulogy,
people she didn't know
listened and cried.

Like her father, she likes the Bible story
about the first in the time of miracles:
the wedding where the Savior
transformed water into wine.

All Those Windowed Rooms

I'm from a city with many bridges—466.
Three more than Venice.
Arch bridges, beam bridges, suspension bridges
life brimmed on both sides of the three rivers.

The hospital I was born in was on the Allegheny.
My father was born along that river too,
but in a house without plumbing or electricity.
His life began in the year of the Great Depression.

When I was a teenager, my middle-aged father
and I parked on the North Side and walked
across the bridge into Pittsburgh. *These are the good*
people, he told me. *People who work hard.*

He wore Brooks Brothers suits, worked
in a glass castle, the PPG building.
I interned at a bank between semesters in college.
I wasn't all grown up, but I dressed like I was.

I'm grown up now. I've moved
to a house on a hill with a river view.
My wordless restlessness matches
the cycle of the seasons.

I marvel at the tide. One minute it looks
like we could walk across the river to town,
then later the same day, the other side is far,
can only be reached by boat or bridge.

There is light in the house. When the windows open,
in the breeze I smell my childhood.
Cut grass. Cherry trees, petals that blanketed
the ground with all they've let go of.

Home Again

Before she leaves each morning, my twenty-four-year-old daughter
pulls the yellow quilt on her childhood bed up to the rumpled pillows.

When she is at work, I smooth, straighten, and tuck in loose corners,
then pick up her stuffed panda and pillow from the floor.

I close every half-opened drawer in her dresser.
I wipe spilled toothpaste from her granite counter.

For her dates, she shops my closet for clothes she seldom returns.
Clothes I don't want back because in reality, they look better on her.

When she does her laundry, she removes mine from the dryer,
heaps it all in a basket on the dining room table for me to fold.

She comes in long past when I fall asleep,
that is if she comes home, and doesn't stay at her boyfriend's.

She has a suitcase in her car at all times. I tell her
it would be more discreet to keep her overnight bag in the trunk.

She rolls her eyes, says, "No one cares—
You have no idea how things are these days."

If she jogs with me, I find my lost eight-minute mile strength,
but then she turns, goes her own way at the stop sign.

If I wake up at 3 a.m., I get out of my bed, crack open
her bedroom door to see if maybe she is home again.

Dora Maar

I forget she was a painter,
a photographer,
an artist, and not simply

a work of art
created by her
clever-with-color lover.

There she sits, framed
flat in her brown chair.

From his eyes to brush—
she's webbed in four sides
of green, yellow, red/orange,
as though she's in a box,

a trick of geometry.
Fingers fan her face,
hold her skull, her cheeks
like a peach full moon. Her breast,

lungs, and heart:
a blue, turquoise, black bouquet,
a stemmed trinity of zero, one, two lines.

Her eyes are different colors,
one green, red the other.
I stare into them.

She is not two-faced;
her nose divides both ways.
Her lips half-smile in profile.

There's an empty white space in her neck—
a void for light or voice—
while her secrets look at me
she turns away from her maker.

If Asked to Give a Commencement Address—The Middle Part

...The fiery marriage between what I know and what I don't know
reminds me of my forty-year vowed commitment to my husband.

We've raised children, buried parents, and kept a canister of dog ashes.
We've woken up on our separate sides of the shared bed and filled days

being who we thought we should be to become who we expected
ourselves to grow into, all the while keeping tallies

and not mastering the math of complicated problem-solving
that takes a whole whiteboard of variables; multiplication,

division, greater-than and less-than signs; and other language of algebra.
Here it's important to add that I suffer

from a chronic tendency to romanticize. The challenge I long
to decipher is my 3:00 a.m. darkness, worry, empty-

place playground for the what-ifs—a litany of what I can't control.
I've been trying to define this space for sixty-five years, all the while

simply stylizing. In current common conversation about you, the younger
generation, my friends—my friends and I share anecdotes about how

our daughters believe someone else, some "influencer" (all that ilk
of self-appointed/self-anointed), someone the young women we raised
listen to.

Whatever we know as mothers can't possibly be true, or work,
or hold any validity. The proof being we don't have millions of followers.

Collecting followers is the credential for wisdom or beauty
or authority of any kind and, therefore, of truth.

We talk, sounding like our own mothers lamenting that nothing
is the same anymore, it's not how it used to be, and it is something

we haven't seen before, so that it's easy to feel untethered, unanchored,
floating far from what we used to know as land.

As I wrote this speech, I looked out my wall of windows and watched
boats flow to the sound and back to the docks where they're moored,

to their homes. The empty places, saved for the vessels to still.
My nighttime angst is often over what I don't or didn't have but wanted.

Different decades, different expectations and hopes: A baby
gave way to healthy children, a shapely figure morphed to lose five pounds...

This list could be as mundane as a sprinkler system; the right color scheme
for drapes, carpet, and upholstery; the balanced ratio of vintage and brand new

to make a house a home; a garden that is mostly perennial peonies and roses
splashed with lush purple petunias and other annuals. I've worked hard

at homemaking. I've devoted days and years to mothering. I've been
a wife through seven different presidents. I'm grandmother of three, soon four.

Yesterday, when the sky was orange, the sun was hidden behind thick air and ozone.
The earth darkened midday due to Canadian wildfires. Every text and conversation

used a phrase like *apocalypse* or *end of the world* or *the Bible said it would be like this.*
Even the lady stocking the condiment aisle at Stop & Shop said, "God's telling us

we better get it right." Later, at a nail salon, I had to wonder, *Is this how I'm going out?*
My last moments of air having a Revlon red gloss painted over my old and thick

toenails. My metatarsals have reshaped themselves with age, like teeth
that need braces. The years show in my skin and ache through my bones.

I am this older woman who watches out windows, one who hadn't imagined
being this version of herself when she was a younger woman still in lockstep

with the magazine ad photos. I listen to podcast reports of NASA discussing skies
full of UFOs, which have been renamed UAP (unidentified aerial phenomena).

And are they coming to destroy us? Or have earthlings done so much
to ourselves and our planet that they are coming to save us? And talk to me, please,

about them because all of my not understanding of myself is only
outweighed by my vast and infinite lack of understanding the other.

Acting Lessons

Pulling up to the gate of her mother's nursing home,
"Hotel California" on the radio, she remembered
another time, when the song came out.

"Begin with *you never gave me...*," her acting coach
directed the lanky blonde she used to be. She was in the center
of the circle of students in his day-long workshop. She cleared
her throat, pushed a loose wisp of hair behind her ear, and began: "You
never gave me," and the words came out about what she wanted, "You
never gave me ballet lessons, you never gave me, you never gave me a
ride, you never gave me protection from his rage."

The actor-turned-teacher watched her face red and contort.

"You never gave me the truth." Her hands shook.

"Now," the teacher said. "Now, say the line."

A Very Brady Renovation

Blended families were not
part of my childhood,
nor was, "Honey, I'm home,"
or a housekeeper making dinner.
Still, in the blue strobe
of my own nighttime loneliness,
I watched the mundane Brady
California dramas—school troubles,
backyard shenanigans,
being a sibling to someone
from a different parent—
the "step" part
of once-removed relationships.
Their living room, kitchen,
bedrooms blended
into a parallel narrative
to my own split-level existence.
So, I wasn't sure if I was awake
last night when the Brady Bunch
reappeared reunited and older.
They used to be my age.
They still are my age.
Now they are characters
on this network I watch for ideas
for how to create, and renovate
homes that outgrow themselves.
Greg, Marsha, and the rest
work side by side with *Good Bones,*
Property Brothers, and *Flea Market Flip.*
Together they demolish the interior
of a 3.5-million-dollar home
that was only ever an exterior.
The reality and sitcom cast
join forces to make real rooms,
with real appliances, electricity,
and toilets where once
was only set design. They remodel
what never really was.
Wallpaper is recreated, as is

Mike Brady's drafting table
where when playing father,
he drew pretend plans.
Episode by episode, everything reappears:
curtains, staircase, the exact
rock wall down to the last stone.
The perfect duplication intoxicates
me with nostalgia and my own list
of the actress I never was,
or the years with the architect
I barely remember,
or the car crash I most regret
and know I can't change.
I weave and untangle
versions, seeds of the delusions
of my younger self.
I wake the next morning
to the hangover
of decades of dwelling
among the emptiness of props.

October Cyclogenesis

At daybreak, despite
winter's early advance
we tend to our routine rhythm—
walk the dog through the mar.
We both wear hats and gloves
the gust shakes branches.
Dead leaves swirl with candy
wrappers, deep puddles ripple.
I try to explain how scared
I get in the dark,
how my heart races.
My husband says, "You're safe."
as if his reminder will make
make me know what I should know.

The back screen door on the empty house
next door blew open and shut.
The "For Sale" sign dangled off its hook.
All the potted ferns have spilled
and the howl won't calm,
even when the sun splits the clouds
and my husband reaches for my cold hand.

Last night, my husband slept
through the worst of the storm
though our dog barked
when the ladder fell
and the garbage splattered.
The shade on our window
swayed with the draft through
the place that no longer closes
in this old house, the part
cracked and not painted shut.
"I'm scared too," I told
our dog as she barked at
what we heard but didn't see.

E=MC Squared

My thoughts ping away
from each unanswered email.
One note says a friend's daughter
was hit by a car. The driver fled.
My turn to respond. Where are the words?

Another message wants
to reach my husband who's traveled
to his hometown to see his friend
who's been hospitalized all winter.

Next email—a real estate link
for the house we sold two years ago—
re-roofed, re-floored, re-staged.
I don't know it anymore.

I vibrate back and forth,
scatter from note to story—
all displaced equilibrium.
My teacher said *E* is energy,
kinetic energy is mass at rest.

In my AARP years of rest,
this tropical landscape
converts my mass.
The variable *E* no longer me—
not the me I know.

That physical entity changed
by some reaction, chemical—
chardonnay on the beach at sunset
my days fade to sherbet sky,
and wait for words from the wave crash.

It's my turn to click reply
though my silence has fused
like hydrogen atoms meld to helium,
triggered at twice the speed of light
into fire called sun and stars.

A Place to Go in Hunger

My grown daughter, the teacher,
asks what's for dinner.
I want to make what she craves,
but my mushroom soup

is an embarrassment
though it's smooth and needs no salt.
At the table we talk, sometimes
tears spill like chicken gravy.

If I were a prophet, I'd know
how a poppy seed blooms red,
but I see only a small black dot.

We slice bread, spread butter.
If I'd learn to listen, I'd know
her stories have answers I forgot.

She talks about new math
and word problems and proofs,
science—all solutions of the natural
world without an equal sign.

She tells me how she feels
when she's not sure
her students understand
the lesson, the riddle—

is X greater than Y
when Y has the most to lose
and X has more to give?

I worry, not if I'm right
or even if I'm wrong,
but when she leaves
the table, is she starved?
Or can I still feed her?

Summary of the Season Finale My Husband Slept Through

I narrate to him that last night both partners
thought they'd given everything up for the other.
It was ugly. They didn't get, they wouldn't get,
what they'd hoped for. I editorialize
that I think rage is clichéd in marriage
after a decade and a half. I sip my coffee, say,
I'm glad we're past those years and continue with the drama—
the husband rattled on about how hard he works,
explained that to work harder
would be impossible. The pretty wife shrieked back
she was a ghost, that's the word she used,
I am a ghost. She never broke out
with her singing career. I sigh in sympathy
for the artist's struggle: If only she didn't have to
raise her family; again, I digress. The handsome husband
(who we, the viewers, know is dead now, in the present day)
shouted well-written lines. His gray hair, wrinkles
and clenched fist made clear he couldn't be enough.
I said to my husband, they should call
this show, *This Is It* instead of *This Is Us*.
It is what it is, it's not what they thought,
or wanted, or thought they wanted.
The characters don't see the big picture,
what we already know—
                                        the loved one will die.

Landscape: Out Loud and in Silence

Daylight smashes my chimeras like ocean waves
smash shell. Being was once inside those sharp carcasses
that make sand painful to walk on. I lift myself
in slow motion. The mind-over-matter doctor says
this pain in my lower back is to distract me
from my repressed emotions—my suppressed unconscious

ocean all stirred and muddy. Some of the restless water
is rain, some poisoned runoff, some high-water table
in this time of saturation. Most of it just melted glacier.
I say, *I love you.* Again. Out loud and in silence.
The atmosphere of our long marriage floods, burns
whole towns. Out our high-rise window, I see the empty
lot that waits. In the meantime, geese dot the grass

and weeds. Cicadas shriek. I can't hear
the sirens or church bells. My ears ring. My only
number is a cell phone, I can't remember the word
to end my thought, then, I can't remember
the thought, but I remember my childhood phone number
memorized like my prayers in case I let go
of my mother's hand, and she couldn't find me.

Awake to 5 a.m. darkness,

I leave
my bed to walk before the golf course
opens. Eyes open, unkept promise of all
I didn't do yesterday. My life morphs.
Each jaunt a hybrid version of my own
duality. My flashlight leads along
the uneven curves of the cart path.
The fairways mowed like clockwork,
chore and pin position a variance
of the sameness of days. Sprinkler
timers trigger arcs to quench the green.
Rakes erase rain divots from sand traps.
My number of steps stay the same. Same
for the number of my miles. The moon
slowly changes from yellow in darkness—
disappeared as orange glow emerges
and blankets branches. Frond patterns form
feathered emptiness where the sky
shows through. Tree frogs at high decibels.
Birds scatter below pink clouds clustered
like confetti. Wings and squawks taunt
my gravity-chained trod. I want to return
North, away from so much heat, but fear
forbids my flight. A waterfall of my worry
crashes. Waves of thought chatter
inside my skull. I miss my kids. Three deer
meet my stare as I pass them. Stoic grace,
not fear, just curious. I am not afraid
of them either, but of my inside world,
where they do not live, I am afraid.
The haunted battle of my failed plans.
Part of me wanders in sync with creatures
from the inlet on the other side. Part of me
circles back to the where I started.

In the Time of Retrograde

What you've always hidden surfaces
like the water from the well
of what we both must swallow—
we are not going backwards, we are barreling
toward that place past our seed. We walk
through our garden not choked with dandelions
and ivy. You and I have weeded.

But there is overgrowth, too much shade,
too little sun. There is cold when the moon
passes between Mercury and us. Our vision
knows the future only from worried hindsight
and our mistakes. It's not retrograde the way
shadow moves over the places we paved,
or above gulfs we found no means
to cross. In this light from far away,
we seem to unwind backward
as we reel ahead toward what is written.

Acknowledgments

I wish to thank the editors of the following journals, where my work has appeared, sometimes in a slightly different version:

AVALON LITERARY REVIEW: *Email to My Dead Father*
BLUESTEM MAGAZINE: *Stockholm Syndrome*
BROAD RIVER REVIEW: *I Can't Tell You Why*
BRICKPLIGHT: *She Thought the Camera Loved Her; Wonder Woman*
CALIFORNIA QUARTERLY (CQ): *Through the Looking Glass*
THE CAPE ROCK: *Recovery Teacher*
CAVEAT LECTOR: *In Another Life*
CIMARRON REVIEW: *You Don't See Me, But I Hear You*
COACHELLA REVIEW: *This is the season boats return* (published as *Friday Before Memorial Day*)
CRITICAL PASS REVIEW: *My Father: Here, Not Here*
DOWN IN THE DIRT MAGAZINE: *All Those Windowed Rooms*
DRUNK MONKEYS: *Summary of the Season Finale My Husband Slept Through*
EDISON LITERARY REVIEW: *Female in a Bot Marriage*
FLIGHTS: *E=MC Squared*
GLASSWORKS: *My Inner Neil Armstrong*
GREEN HILLS LITERARY LANTERN: *Not in the Wonder Box*
JOKES LITERARY REVIEW: *If Asked to Give a Commencement Address—The Middle Part*
THE MEADOW: *Landscape: Out Loud and in Silence*
MOON CITY REVIEW: *October Cyclogenesis*
THE OPIATE: *The Fire We Spin Around; Truth, Beauty and Photoshop*
OPEN: JOURNAL OF ARTS & LETTERS: *Not Found in Obituaries, Eulogies, Fairy Tales, or the Book I Haven't Written*
ORIGINS JOURNAL: *About the Life You Imagine for Yourself*
PENNSYLVANIA ENGLISH: *Born to Pittsburgh*
THE PHOENIX SOUL: *Detours*
PINK PANTHER MAGAZINE: *Writing the Part of Her Father*
PISGAH REWVIEW: *A Life Review: Four Stars* (originally published as *A Review from Heaven to My Children*)
THE POTOMAC REVIEW: *Untraveled*
RED WHEELBARROW REVIEW: *A Place to Go in Hunger*
RUBBERTOP REVIEW: *The Notion of Being Prepared*
SCHUYLKILL VALLEY REVIEW: *Every Night, I'm Lying in Bed Holding You Close in My Dreams*

SEQUESTRUM: *Acting Lessons*
STONECOAST REVIEW: *Zero-Sum Game*
TERMINUS: *Pittsburgh as a Metaphor for My Father; The Morning My Father Moved into Assisted Living*
THIRD WEDNESDAY: *Dora Maar*
TOWN CREEK POETRY: *Lost Along the Way*
VIRGINIA NORMAL: *Outline for Her Novel*
VISITANT: *Mutated World Sequence*
VOICES DE LA LUNA: *Imagined Future*

Cathy Allman writes from Naples, FL and Norwalk, CT where she lives with her husband. She has been widely published in dozens of literary journals, including *Cimarron Review, Moon City Review, The Potomac Review*, and *Terminus*. She has an MFA from Manhattanville University. Her poem "Not in the Wonder Box" was nominated for a Pushcart Prize. *All Those Windowed Rooms* is her debut collection. Visit cathyallman.com.

www.ingramcontent.com/pod-product-compliance
Lightning Source LLC
LaVergne TN
LVHW090536110826
845146LV00003B/1129

* 9 7 9 8 8 9 9 9 0 4 8 4 4 *